ARDOUR

NICOLE BROSSARD

TRANSLATED BY ANGELA CARR

COACH HOUSE BOOKS | TORONTO

We acknowledge the financial support of the Government of Canada
through the National Translation Program for Book Publishing, an initiative
of the Roadmap for Canada's Official Languages 2013–2018: Education,
Immigration, Communities, for our translation activities. Published with
the generous assistance of the Canada Council for the Arts and the Ontario
Arts Council. Coach House Books also acknowledges the support of the
Government of Canada through the Canada Book Fund.

LIBRARY AND ARCHIVES CANADA CATALOGUING IN PUBLICATION

Brossard, Nicole, 1943-
[Ardeur. English]
        Ardour / Nicole Brossard ; Angela Carr, translator.

Translation of: Ardeur.
Poems.
ISBN 978-1-55245-322-3 (paperback).

    I. Carr, Angela, 1976-, translator II. Title. III. Title: Ardeur. English.

PS8503.R7A7613 2015   C841'.54   C2015-905046-4

Ardour is available as an ebook: ISBN 978 1 77056 420 6

Purchase of the print version of this book entitles you to a free digital copy.
To claim your ebook of this title, please email sales@chbooks.com with
proof of purchase or visit chbooks.com/digital. (Coach House Books
reserves the right to terminate the free digital download offer at any time.)

think of your life without it
— Anne Carson

what would difference be
a repeated gesture
in the shadow of the species
what would it usually be
in a moment our mouths
if we could make out
my side our side
in the hollows of living languages

who said that to burn
relieves matter or emptiness
anger or me or you
who did not say melancholy
at point-blank range
in the sounding of time

it's that life devours
characters and carapaces
the whole dream
the capacity for dialogue

now that you've said
to dream in the midst of *toujours*
uproots presence instead
today the unnameable
dispels the idea of classifying
humanity in its multitude
and salty vertigo

at the edge of the abyss the business of hope
all that i'm watching for
inwardly we say raw consolation
bush of traditions embracing the cities' youthful names
sprout of feline strength
let's stay close to our roots
proficient with knots and ardour

regarding dogs let's say
barking wanders
we are here to speak
in the multitude of wounds
mouths and clean-sweeping pronouns
in the darkness an intoxicating
slowness and immobility

ardour the question of ardour
the hand's movement
the aerial movement of intoxication
pastel soul tint
let's try to side with the sobbing
immerse our ardour
in questions and cherries

this way of staying in the shadow
scarlet mouth bursting with names
today
i acquiesce
let's make time for torment
eyes yearning for the wind

round number of sensations
when it is necessary i age
in verbless sentences
attentive to the rocks' pink profile
before the sea
and all the oxygen, the archives

hazelnut shadow in september
there will be there was
always ignorance
who should i embrace this morning
between changing affections
and the hard pits of words

something like wait for me
in the braille of scars
tonight can i suggest a little punctuation
circle half-moon vertical line of astonishment
a pause that transforms
light and breath
into language and threshold of fire

a desire to bite into abundance
of sincere selves between books and screens
i say so to hold on until morning
with clipped words
at dawn an ellipse raised like an eyebrow

let's awaken night in its familiar curve
awaken gestures as if we're about to enter
history and cafés
at full speed seeming powerful
we escape time
vanishing point embedded in our mirrors

rare are the books that sweep across
the back of dawn
from a word
small horizon of pain that tramples

small click rose flavour a single question

between kisses

now no one can clearly recall

the colour of silence

before the alphabets intersected

and the former purpose of melancholy's curtains

i stay out of reach
with no one around murmuring
or counting the bones the cruelty
by instinct i roll in dark matter
i smooth the heat

i want all tastes to last
in nature, crab claws
urchins ready to roll on in fiction
at any time of day and in darkness
silence of starting again

then i find myself turning my back on the planets
depending on the sounds of intimate speech or to say
farewell following the light
schools of sardines of dolphins of sharks
struggling with dawn drowning i find myself
retracing the flow of time
gaze blurred
by the breakneck speed of the universe

for the sea's blue wounds
and embraces i wanted
to chart slow responses
the true obscurity of absence's gaps
to translate in circular dreams repetitions
the horizon line
for each generation

on a small scale
what fascinates
if not repetition
the same *us* divided
among the paradoxes
of art and the illiterate density
of hands and guns
dark cell
knife to the throat
the world carries on
we bid each other farewell
eyelids slowing
between apparitions

so i'm not getting used to the darkness
of soldiers and archives
i don't know in what order
to recount civilization's opacity
the grey taste of excess consumption

what can i say not to harm
the future and not to trample beyond
let's go: old abyss of the horizon

noon behind the nape
torrent of griefs and sparks
the voice regains its rhythm on the threshold
of immobility
my nature between two sentences
how to appease with a single gesture
whoever cries fully in darkness

toward what angle of destruction are we going
to remember to lift tenderness
night's curtain
a diagonal before forgetfulness?

we call it sound of beauty
the sea fused with salt
in the neverending night
beyond all narratives
we also call
sound of beauty the silence
its slow signature at the bottom of dawn

that night we said it
centuries of metaphor would go
on the same impulse be stranded ashore
on crumbling landscapes
our muscles suddenly trembling
to recall the word of mouth
old language trotting
in the coolness so long sought
in eternity's paragraphs

magic of crossing bridges
menu fragment of hereafter
who are we
to desire still
across metaphors of collision
contrasts in fleeting silk of dawn and joy

it's not wise
to say devour or burn
directly from our pink existence
it's not wise
to join a civilization
of butchers and inquisitors

of course, there are the missing
women who loved
children, museums, olives
our civilization a little
but above all hope with its
paradoxes and perpetual life
of course all that's in the future
i must imagine it sincere hands
undo it, start again
not so much rage or death
vertiginous slope
in the middle, life, grand cru

how dare say again
my core drowned among syllables
and believe to light thus
the fecund slope of the other me
her arms tireless with creation

bestiality equivocates dying
and its vocabulary full of debris
who then wants to drown the carcass
a great cry, not the night

always the fervour of culture transforms
the species within us, deploys it
speech recumbent in our joints
from far away we say: that's the planet

thousands of works backs turned to night
thousands of unclassifiable gestures
in the oceans' depths and in the contours of war
thousands of bodies and we want abbreviations?

but i am vast
when all is pounding slaughter within us

we are alive to the very end
with the idea of kissing
and in the head tirelessly
humanity humid hurricane
such opulence and its abyss

we are still there book in hand
it's afternoon, we should
speak of the present in miniature
reflect on the details
human remains or abundance
acquiesce if someone trembles

we are still there
it's insensitive
to ask these questions
of memory and the absolute
it's insensitive
to drown in dawn
as many faces
and breathing
in light time
all this violence that comes
to the tips of fallen arms

hands below the nape
it's the least of things
to say see you tomorrow comparing
the century and collected nights
let's start again: i'm flexible

Napes

in all of us there's a silence
that gallops on nights of sorrow

Nape 1

to be this body in the breakneck speed of the present
brushing against
grief when touching
the other's gestures and their petals
of memory and shimmering

and before the 'bad infinity'
we embrace without hesitation
to impress
the animal leap
an impassive glance
in our chests

Nape 2

no need to
fold up in dice of fiction to escape
the speed of torment
if chance fragments
such long sounds from throat and darkness
language exiting an obsession

Nape 3

in the great fishbowl of murmurs and all
that breathes
echoing civilization i want
utopia to forget nothing
to stay within reach of Pompeii
amid secrets and when it's timely
to descend softly

Nape 4

dictionary in hand, i can
submerge my soul in all my cities
of origin
utter blue or death
in another language
i am not afraid of disappearing
i know how to circulate between centuries
to classify the flavours of saffron and salt

so each time it's half
a life of turned pages
a nice shot of emptiness in certitude

Nape 5

how is it that prose astonishes the mouth
of someone who is no longer quite someone
just a melody in an ideal
real place
capable of infiltrating
secrets and reflected collisions

Nape 6

inside/outside
the infinite an eddy of numerals and light
lace of constellations
inside/outside
matter keeps watch
salt of patience and of hybrid memory
our tiny animals from childhood

Nape 7

now thoughts emerge
from light and its fragile frescoes
the body's temperature equal/s
breath/e emotion
then we focus on disasters
and overeat

Nape 8

fragments, someone says it's difficult
the muscled back of death
men and sea monsters
vigorous horses still more
dragons, a lion that swallows
livinggallopofmelancholy
water spurting from shadow and duration
slow water bottomless with symbols
it's over there Piazza Navona
from latin until us, the night remembers

Nape 9

in our thoughts here are the slow organs
of memory, surely our fugitive
imagination recaptured among
crowds and given names
she loves fervour without any erasure
all the way to the temples
ramifying senses and caresses
all forms of kissing combined

Nape 10

whirlwind i also love
the species knotted in dog days and *l'intimité*
the very depths of respiration
our 'us' enumerated flaming new

Nape 11

i am as pronounced
language or war or premature
soon turning to the north
its adjectives of ice and the present
soon thrown free a sentence
in the light of comparisons
i become again a piece of time
embedded in our species

Nape 12

back, ankles, everything has a name
ephemeralawn vertigo
everything has a name
minuscule come my life
in the short duration of replies
go look further
still a little ink a dénouement

Dice. Square of night.
Now beyond the barbed wire
come, i put my hand on your waist.

Nape 13

in the search for etymology everything changes
pencils questioning
the dark the charcoal
Dürer's drawings imbuing
a myth in each face
a new species, fog
already told, already linked
prepared to be taken away
in the fragile foreignness
of dawn and lucidity

Nape 14

an orange at breakfast, a clock
deep in the heart
in the labyrinth of hot blood, we can create
down to the smallest detail
dense leaves of a notebook
a cricket's cry or screeching metal
then fear of hope in the middle of a sentence
gain the riverbank and narrate
until sated

Nape 15

at least two adjectives are needed
before taking a seat at the window
to observe then if tenderness
if infinity or someone in the garden
stretched nape relieved of chaos

Nape 16

all of a sudden a sky of questions
rain out of range
between eyelashes two or three murmurs
warmth ankles
multiple birthmarks
in the same place
without verging on the word *chaos*
without summary the blood rushes to the head
until dawn
our non-fall in the dark

rain hollering, everything goes

Nape 17

when you reverse the nature of thoughts said
to be of disarray
an imperfect tense suffices to say it was so beautiful
that day
no one hid from caresses
throat tight or face drowning in storms

Nape 18

the non-description of happiness
in each era
voluminous vocabulary disperses us in time
starting with the first treatises on catastrophe
and the West

other times at night, i know
this certainty is not new
allurement

Nape 19

the noise of blazing fires
questions, art
eyelids, murmur of infinitesimal goodbyes
still i listen on language's frontiers
the familiar sound as we dive into thirst
melancholy drowning in a fervour for origins

Nape 20

right from the beginning *quel sourire*
materials of shadow and the universal
for art yes draw well
its *éternité* its most beautiful scars
heart captive of noise of cages of the other
at any moment it is widely known
languages trembling

Nape 21

i saw you thinking all that
humanity in a gesture
alterity

night's equilibrium
we are in architecture

Nape 22

across ink
to each fiction
one fewer pain

so quiet so hot
it's a shadow
without crowds

Nape 23

all that is simple
joyous like a Lambrusco
in April in Montréal
when everyone speaks
of their mother with a suitcase
as before birth
moving with her body of fresh water
in former times and fluidity

Nape 24

you've been lying down
in lost time and reading again
and the universe. You see tenderness
come at the moment of awakening
and comparisons, yet night
fragments of words and *fucking chaos*
in your body there was the excess noise
of fate and schrapnel
always about to roll in the chest
and morning

Nape 25

we know that the word *century* intoxicates birds
decorates ruins
and freezes us in abandonment
we all have lives that can spin
to the sea
with inward tops
the ends of strings hanging
sentences that touch us a little
some days as to rain, as to death

Nape 26

you walk among adult landscapes
night of tombs and daturas
thoughts full
of small flags and bursting fruit
their way of separating
in the mouth of childhood and the reason
for crowds

Nape 27

therefore someone thought
of images, accounted for
the continents, therefore someone knows
why the interior
muscles, breath and the heart surpass
the intentions of dawn and voracity

Nape 28

while night rolls
its artifice and screen *climax*
on the backdrop of a virtual city tonight
i can
say: *in my lifetime* the earth

i can also
squander *my life* in the irreality of words
repeat in my lifetime
i can see everything transforms
bodies pressed peacefully to night we must
re-immerse ourselves in absence

Nape 29

i would have liked to say that
with concrete words
the background of reality

say: this is my suitcase
here is the Terrace of the Lions
i am drinking lemonade beside a river

i would have also liked the helping words, night that falls
no pain
i can't understand everything

be with only my mouth
all space

Shadow: Soft and Soif

i'm careful not to disappear
on the other side of my dreams
the method: to plummet
voice, face profiled in air
quick to dive into a gifted language

a few syllables more
to the bottom of the mirror
we are already there

i have not yet spoken
of disappearance nor of vocabulary it's too vast
and you remember solitude
scrapes the bottom of the sea and the alphabet
so that night can reach across the invisible
all the way to
our notebooks of resistance

for the time being don't forget
to regulate immensity
to space out everything that brings you to tears
the silence in light obstinately

for the time being
we must tell
night falls slowly

we saw life rise

high among the installations

colour transform itself

into tiger and origin

behind the window

we learned

to foil the idea of truth

in the dark and otherwise

yet here life falls
night on your breast
while civilizations flow
and *word* is a word
used for rubbing lucidity
against dawn and the shadow
cast by no one

as to the number of poems, i always knew
if someone was going to die
or touch dawn
with their mouth or tomorrow

about stars: we tended to
regard them with distress and exactitude
the universe could have suddenly transformed itself into
avalanche
broken glass and voice. Music
or farewell to perfection.

don't forget
we must tell
night falls slowly

Life, *la vie n'était pas dure.*
It was July and we were
lost to work. Night
i said yes in the lips' darkness
red reason reviving the present
vowels trembling.

Today the air is opaque and clinking:
an erosion of symbols
the world in plain sight of our eyes.
Morning, I count
roses, insects. And solitude.
Hiding my sighs
I drown easily in the urban wind
verb tenses and your hair.
Feuillage dense d'origine.

outside the framework, joy in silhouette
i touch all *life follows its course*
a stone that endures, a child
a mirrored sound
and not necessarily a smile

in reality space thins
ardour draws its knots of presence
here and there in the city we live
on convictions yes and azure
we have dark hair
and our seductions vibrate valiant repetitions
in the gardens and parks take note
the words will soon come   there
to tear you from the simple present of the abyss

across the foliage of words
a few night syllables
let's watch
our dream muscles move
eyes outdistanced by nostalgia
we watch
tears, palms and fists like thirst
and the idea that living is
necessarily all *à l'intérieur du langage*

since the wind sweeps across
both the horizon and breasts
in the rain sometimes there's no one
or a face in disorder
a mouth that exaggerates
all agape
at the end it's magnificent
night trembles like a fruit tree
a danger

some days a blow
of violence a blow of murmurs
the stories pile up
you observe the bodies

                    r
i repeat   o   n
we long to be t   from
the simple present of the abyss

it's yes: at nightfall
pain awakens carnivorous
rolls more nobly
quick under the tongue

yet there will be no portrait
of my mother, no etching or gesture
in language that flounders
there will be only a scene
still standing in the city and the wind
a beastly melancholy that dawn
will seize from speed and intensity

i won't write *wound*
and all the gestures that pool
at the end of the sentence

and don't complain
if shadow adds contour to reality
like at the cinema
if it's dark and hazy
between eyelashes and time

to be for a whole life in the changeable species
with this reflex that persists in wanting
to represent everything, euphoria, gestures
bites, rooms with their hollows
shadow and softness, worried foreheads
our fragility
of course, we are speechless with
every kiss

heat that whispers near the temples
fictions of dawn and the absolute
i like any night that moves the knees

i also noted this:
night inverts the horizon
but how does it become so silky
among the nebulæ without protection
entangled with the pain of the horizon
and softness that blazes in the voice

ideas of the fall and the labyrinth
as if at the tips of our arms
all that exists was
for a day made to move dawn
raise the curtain on the animal kingdom

so i keep watch
among knives and dust

i have not yet spoken of disappearance
before the pronouns
life makes decisions
under the skin
makes a dream wheel, hoops
math games and caskets

now here are the glaciers
some materials
from dawn and suffering

dawn does not darken
it has upper-case letters
can elegantly juxtapose
vivid smiles
and wounds, if you'd like

mornings the flooded planet
when the universe shoves you in the back
if you want other sensations
don't let reality
decide. Dive

every time the future emerges
in a word, a woman's belly
life's thirst overwhelms breathing

let her stream

in the world's dew
under the feverish fingernail

and if torment if what stirs
your nights of reading and irreality
si la poussière sur tes doigts vibre
lean on the shadow
in a place that's blue or the void
for sure there will be water in your eyes
modernity and fear in your attire

then in the room *nape* returns
as a word we must imagine
the hours
their trailing curve in the heights of thought
drone adrift overhead

everything changes so
the world is thus constructed
destruction repeats itself
illumination *le* dark in our eyes

or sound of night here
slow step of desire
in our chests heat
blazing hearth
under the pink of the fingernail, and tomorrow

it's true, when together we often
want to undress the world
make sense of life by touching
drawn closer because of farewells
tragedies, all that's unspeakable

softly no nothingness
just a story of *toss a coin*
along the everyday
with fabulous and futuristic creatures
ready for the intoxication of language and eternity
acrobats suspended
by our need for the ocean and distance

remain firmly in silence
at dawn the verb *to be* rushes
in the veins, heavenly body it courses
as after love or a grain of salt
on the tongue in the morning, taste of immensity
or light in the breaking waves of time
it returns us to
the first dampness
come hold me
think about water's great power
that makes a place of us

it will have been
an idea of flight and passion
light in breaking waves of time
sea as volume
in the alphabet and the present

Nicole Brossard is a poet, novelist and essayist who has published more than forty books since 1965, including many that have been translated into English: *These Our Mothers, Lovhers, Mauve Desert, Museum of Bone and Water, Notebook of Roses and Civilization, Fences in Breathing* and *Selections: The Poetry of Nicole Brossard,* among others. She co-founded *La Barre du Jour* and *La Nouvelle Barre du Jour,* two important literary journals in Québec. She has won two Governor General's Awards for poetry, as well as le Prix Athanase-David and the Canada Council's Molson Prize. In 2010, she was made an Officer of the Order of Canada and in 2013 chevalière de l'Ordre national du Québec. In 2013, she received le Prix international de littérature francophone Benjamin Fondane. She lives in Montréal.

Angela Carr is a poet and translator. Her most recent book is *Here in There.* Originally from Montréal, she currently lives in New York City.

Typeset in Amethyst. Amethyst is an old-style type drawn by Jim Rimmer for his Pie Tree Press in New Westminster, B.C. Rimmer based the idea on a set of roman capitals he drew in 1994 under the title Maxwellian, which were not released for commercial use but rather as a private type for his press. The letterforms are a product of Rimmer's calligraphic touch, much in the same light as his Albertan family.

Printed at the Coach House on bpNichol Lane in Toronto, Ontario, on Zephyr Antique Laid paper, which was manufactured, acid-free, in Saint-Jérôme, Quebec, from second-growth forests. This book was printed with vegetable-based ink on a 1965 Heidelberg KORD offset litho press. Its pages were folded on a Baumfolder, gathered by hand, bound on a Sulby Auto-Minabinda and trimmed on a Polar single-knife cutter.

Edited by Alana Wilcox
Designed by Alana Wilcox
Cover by Zab Design and Typography

Coach House Books
80 bpNichol Lane
Toronto ON M5S 3J4
Canada

416 979 2217
800 367 6360

mail@chbooks.com
www.chbooks.com